The Alchemy of Love

Words and Images

Nadine Gay

ISBN: 1461001080
ISBN-13: 9781461001089

To Dave
and all peaceful warriors of the heart

CONTENTS

ACKNOWLEDGMENTS

Writing is a solitary act; the production of a book is a collective endeavor. It takes the talent of many to bring it to fruition. This book is no exception, and I want to express my gratitude to all who made it possible. Barbara Terrell, my brilliant editor, who shaped this collection of poems; I couldn't have done this without you. Thank you, my twin, for your review and your encouragement; our epistolary relationship inspired me to put down my thoughts, perceptions and feelings. Gratitude to my dear friend, Marilyn King, who offered to proofread the manuscript. You did a peerless job, and I used many of your valuable suggestions. Adrian Curtet, my son and a talented digital artist who designed the book cover and the title pages, a zillion thanks. I am so proud of you. And finally, I can't begin to express my gratitude to Dave, my partner, for his contributions, his support, his inspiration and love.

FOREWORD

THE WORDS

Robert Frost once wrote, "A poem begins as a lump in the throat, a sense of wrong, a homesickness, a lovesickness." The poems in the opening section (The Alchemy of Love) of this new collection by Nadine Gay reflect the latter, capturing the essence of deeply felt emotions and accompanying passion. They begin with self-questioning, move to a resolve to embrace possibilities, and then describe the journey that love takes us on. If we have been fortunate enough to experience love, Ms. Gay's intimate and personal journey leads us, inexorably, to familiar and recognizable terrain.

Since Ms. Gay is also a highly gifted visual artist, it is no wonder that her poems are filled with distilled and colorful images, as in "Sunrise" in the section entitled Haikus of Sorts. One is easily swept into her world—a world that, like her sculptures and paintings, evokes nature as the physical manifestation of spirituality. In her poems, an intensely felt moment or image is laid bare before us, celebrating an atavistic, harmonic connection to the earth as well as to each other. There is an unmistakable Native American sensibility in her appreciation for, and depiction of, nature.

In the final section, Small Tales, her life experiences and observations reveal alternating glimpses of her delight in the well-captured moment ("The Night I Spent with Maurice Sendak") and of her more serious reflections in poems such as "Grief." As facets of her exquisitely drawn and "lived" worldview, these vignettes exemplify both a transparency of being as well as an understanding of the gravitas of the human condition. If "style is the man" (woman, in this case), then her writing faithfully comes across as truthful and real. Her expressive domain abandons any need for artifice or guile.

Nadine Gay's poems are at once intimate and universal, captivating in their insights, and reassuring in their openness and acceptance. They are fine examples of the interrelated creative force in love, art and nature.

Barbara Terrell

THE IMAGES

The archetypal themes of quest and transformation are also inherent in Ms. Gay's artwork. Her paintings and sculptures meld the human experience with natural elements. The viewer is captured by the complexity of intermingled images and wonders about the gravity of slightly submerged symbolism. Each piece seems to seek compassion in the midst of oblique mysteries.

In "A Lover's Journey," corvid spirit-guides track lovers' uncharted flight against a watercolor backdrop of cosmic night and swirling ether. In "Firebird," winged creatures breathe life into sleeping souls. Ready to ride into the unknown, "The Horse Dreamer" reflects a yearning for the intangible. Abstract paintings such as "The Wave" or "Teepees" mix colors with bleeding edges and constant motion, reflecting the joyous dance of existence.

One cannot quickly absorb any of Nadine Gay's work. It is rich with layers and levels of meaning to be unraveled. Slowly, her poems and visual art draw you into their dream world, a place where connecting with yourself and the collective unconscious becomes possible.

Dave Stoebel

INTRODUCTION

I have been a passionate reader since that magical moment when letters coalesced to tell a story. I still remember that moment with amazing clarity, the enchantment and awe at the opening of my world.

I didn't always know that I wanted to be an artist. When I attended high school in France, I studied a lot of left-brain stuff, such as science and mathematics. I was no wizard, but I was pretty good at it, and I passed my Baccalaureat [French exit exam] in math and physics.

After graduating from high school, I enrolled at the university, majoring in biology. A couple of months later, I quit. The course of my life didn't feel right, but I had no idea what did.

I left France, lived on a kibbutz, traveled around for a year, worked odd jobs and ended up in New York City in the fall of 1974. Another year passed and then, suddenly, I knew what I wanted to do -- I wanted to study art. I enrolled at CCNY and then transferred to Pratt Institute. I had found my path, or maybe it had found me.

I have been making art ever since, and it is such an integral part of me that I cannot imagine doing anything else.

Poetry came into my life more recently. Reading Mary Oliver a few years ago, I felt an urge to write. To my surprise, I found that poetry seemed to flow onto the page with relative ease and, most importantly, that writing gave me immense pleasure.

My visual art and writing are intimate explorations of my inner worlds. My meditation practice of many years helps me find a center of stillness. That quiet place makes it possible for me to accept whatever is in the moment and find the courage to stand naked, communicating the unique reckoning of my own human experience. Somehow, in that fearless stepping in, something beyond the self comes through.

I don't like to explain my visual art. The work unfolds, reveals itself. Often, I don't know why certain images appear. While I write poems with more conscious intent and accessibility, my aim is that both expressions become portals through which you can step and thereby create your own stories.

WATERCOLORS

Clear transparent water on the thick paper invites the brush to dissipate its saturated hues. Hardly touching the surface, it dances -- the hand merely an instrument. No thoughts, no plans, only colors melting, blending, working their magic.

Before me, like cloud formations, lies a play of shapes and colors. Here is a dragon about to swallow a rabbit. There is a woman kneeling, her hands becoming tree branches.

Details are painted to define images. I follow a waking dream, my half-opened eyes Japanese lanterns floating on a subterranean stream of consciousness. Staying out of the way is my main assignment.

The paintings unfold. They disclose the barely audible whisper of our interconnectedness with elemental forces, with the primordial energy called love. They are footprints of transformation calling you to make your own.

Firebird

Black Bird's Dream

Woman's World

Lover's Journey

Part One

The Alchemy of Love

Fast Train

I am on a fast train to nowhere.
Soft eyes are required
to see the blurred edges
of fly-by telephone poles,
of cows nonchalantly grazing,
of rushing trees,
of vanishing houses.

Pulled inward by the relentless motion,
I remember coming to you
grinning in the face of danger,
wild hair framing my forehead,
my armor discarded.

I reflect on the pledge,
made not long ago,
to fling myself into life
not knowing if she would catch me,
but unwilling to remain
on the sidelines.

As the train speeds on,
my reflection superimposed
on a strip of sky, dotted with white clouds
sweeping past me with unseemly velocity,
I know
there is no other way
but to plunge into the silt of our humanity
pregnant with all there is:
the pain and the sorrow, the longing and the joys,
the ecstasy and the doubts, the fear and the trust
and most of all
the love,
that harmonic resonance,
with its tender fierceness,
its unwavering demand of selflessness,

stripping us of everything
except the ardent yearning
to be filled
with glorious light.

For then and only then,
we might chance to experience
the simple transparency of being
that comes from fearless surrender.

When Love Comes

When love comes,
I will greet her with open arms
and let her fierce wings
beat without restraint
against my ribs.

When love comes,
I will jump into her raging storm,
feet first, eyes wide open,
her unfettered wind
hurling me into the blazing skies.

When love comes,
a wild horse,
black as night,
her mane strewn with shooting stars,
I will leap upon her fleeing back
and ride, ride, ride as far as eternity....

When love comes,
I will remember my forgotten name.

Transformation

I go through the day
with an empty space
oblong in shape,
skin and bones dissolved
from my chest to my belly,
the whole world passing through ~
a car
a child
a rosy cloud
a wrinkled face
the bursting trees
a mother sitting on a bench
the wind
a song
your smile
your eyes
your hand reaching for my heart
only to find liquid light.

And all the while,
I smile.

Dancing

I am dancing with my beloved,
on a Sunday afternoon,
to a tender song
carried by the breeze,
his hand gently holding mine.
Our bodies,
outlined by threads of light,
sway.
The melody winds through our hearts.
Love shines.

Visitation

In the depth of the night,
unbidden,
my dark lover
slips beneath the covers.
Long fingers tangled in my hair
pull me from
the frayed edges
of dreamless sleep.

He murmurs raspy vowels
into my ear,
an arcane alphabet
lifted from
the Dead Sea Scrolls.

From his tongue,
a string of runes tumbles
into my mouth.
I taste the mossy green
of ancient tree groves.
His hand slowly travels
the length of my thighs
patiently decoding
the velocity of desire,
encrypted
in the fragile equation of our bodies.
There is no telling where this will end…

An upside down moon
hangs in the window-framed sky.

Desire Dreams

Are the purple shadowed trees nearby
dreaming me
across the continent,
so that I may sail
the length of your body
to drink from your lips
the warmth of sleep?

Have the ocean of the East
and the ocean of the West
conspired to pause
on the crest of our breaths,
so that we may taste
their briny mist
from each other's tongues?

The bony fingers of your ribs
have loosened their grip,
just enough, for
the moon,
that temptress of lovers,
to flood your cavity
with an uncanny glow.
Swirling spirals of moonlight
curl into a perfect nest
and I,
sometimes a swallow,
sometimes a raven,
mostly always in flight,
come to rest there
just for an instant
head under wing.

Heartbeat after heartbeat
pounding,
desire dreams of desire.

Your thighs enclose
a sea that swells
with secret tides
and swallows the stars
one by one.

At the body's edge,
there is a river
always flowing backward
into a past already here,
and a future
that circles round and round
threading our wing bones together
into a peculiar sculpture
that only we can see.

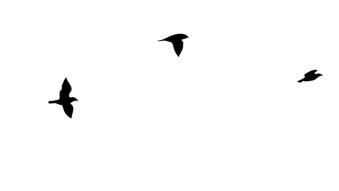

Ecstasy

A joy almost
   too great to bear.
      Molecules are forced
         into
new constellations
   until now
      unimagined.

At the call of your voice
   my soul leaps,
      fearless
         into
the void
   and lands
      on a passing star.

Could it be
   a fragment of your heart?

We Peaceful Warriors of the Heart

We are clouds in an endless sky
We are smiles in the face of danger
We are pauses between breaths
We are tender hands caring for the sick
We are kisses on our children's foreheads
We are dewdrops on velvety petals
We are shoulders to cry on
We are feet rushing to help
We are wrinkles on the faces of our elders
We are the rain on the parched earth
We are wings light as feathers
We are eyes that see through darkness
We are songs of the Bewick's wren
We are tears for those who cannot cry
We are the wind stirring the wild oats
We are the silence between the notes
We are lotuses on a quiet pond
We are lovers joined in bliss

We peaceful warriors of the heart
have lost our names
and found our home.

The Alchemy of Love

From blood-filled muscle
pumping oxygen
to my earthly body,
my heart has become a kite
lit by dawn's vivid hues.
It flies through
ever-changing skies,
borrowing the fleece of fluffy clouds
to fashion a scarf
that will keep us warm
through the inevitable storms.

Its tail of tears and smiles
is tied in bright ribbons,
lifted from
gossamer rainbows.
It traces
the capricious movements of the wind,
trailing in its wake
flocks of swallows, wrens and meadowlarks --
a flurry of beaks and feathers.

These heavenly messengers
will soon have need of rest.
One by one they will settle
in the soft hollow of
our arms' inviting nest,
and dream their bird dreams,
folded wing over beak.

Nighttime

All night your arm
rests across my chest
bridging my right shoulder
to my left one.
My heartbeat pulsates
under the arch
of your silken skin.

I am anchored
amidst a sea
of rising desires.
The waves' foamy tongue
ebbs around my breasts
barely brushing
the tips of my nipples.

Awakening from a deep slumber,
you slide effortlessly
into the delta
of my thighs
and travel
the depth of my body
carried
by the marine breeze
and the moon's irresistible pull.
The bed creaks
with the weight of
passion shaken loose.

Somewhere in the distance
a foghorn sounds,
and together,
holding tight,
we ride
on the backs of silvery dolphins,
returning to the source of time,
before the birth of stars.

Homage to Elizabeth B.

[and those of us who can't help but have romantic hearts...]

How do I love thee? Let me count the ways...

I love thee by candlelight when night is wrapped tightly around us.
I love thee with a presence that makes seconds spill into the hourglass of eternal grace.
I love thee with words that write themselves onto the empty page.
I love thee to the edge of being, when looking back, I see nobody's waiting.
I love thee with the brightest magenta, yellow and cobalt my brush can hold.
I love thee with mercurial feet that bring me, with one step, wherever you are.
I love thee with a quiet certitude as simple as a straight line drawn through a circle.
I love thee for no reason at all.

Remembering

Remembering
the feel of you,
the weight of you,
the taste of you.
Zero degrees of separation.
Durga whirling,
Krishna dancing,
bodies merging.
Gliding through the night,
breathing you in,
breathing you out,
skin always touching.
The warmth of you,
the warmth of me,
the lightest brush of lips,
hands on skin.
Reaching in,
reaching out,
delighted in your delight,
in you delighting me.
The edge of pleasure
unraveling,
raw sensations,
reconfiguring molecules.
DNA spiraling outward.
    A burst of rapture-
    shattered splendor-
Turned inside out.

Dawn slipping through the shades.
Strands of faint light weaving us
into the softest light blue sky.
The whole universe
holding us.
Reborn.

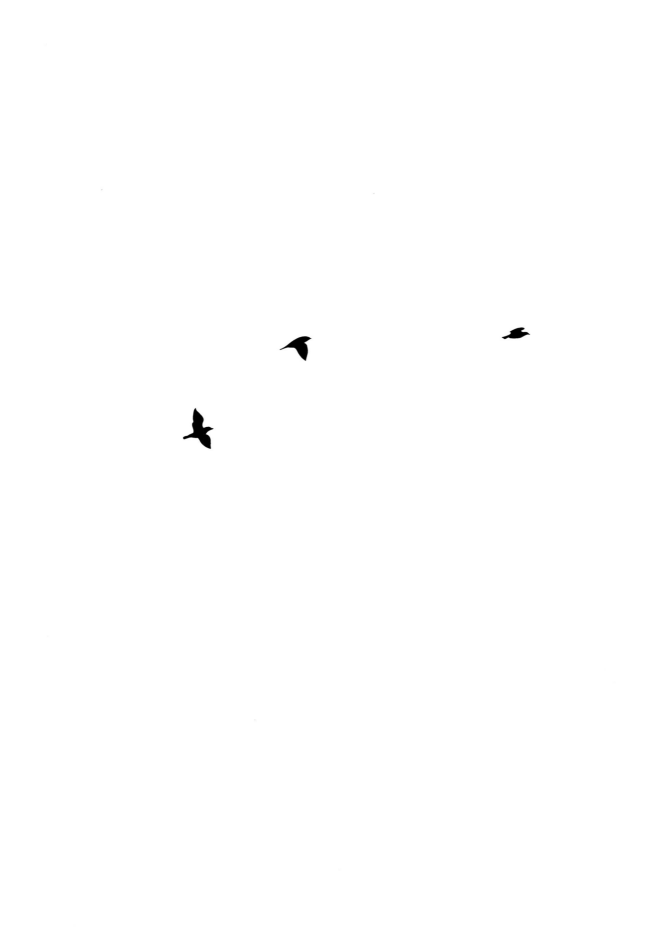

ABSTRACTIONS

Sometimes they are tossed shapes on paper,
sometimes, wild strokes of the laden brush,
at other times a cheerful dance of lines and circles.

Abstractions are playful and spontaneous expressions
of form and color.

They call forth the undiluted delight
of the child seeing the world
for the first time.

Teepees

Two Moons

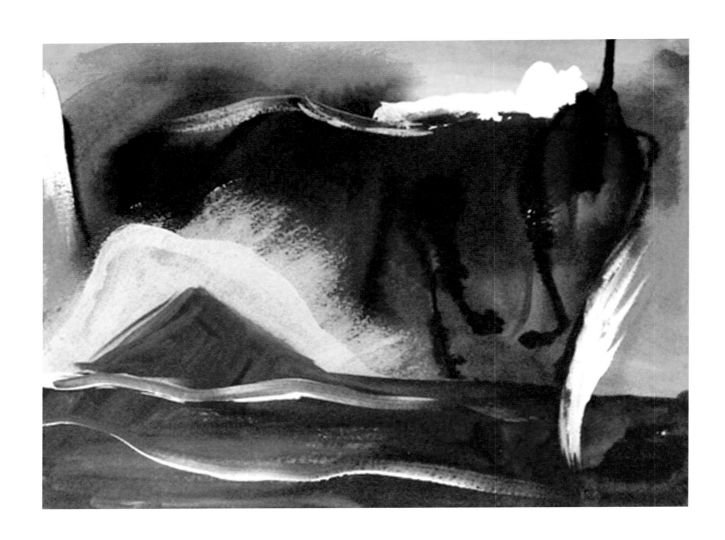

Wave

Vista

Part Two

Haikus of Sorts

Stillness

Against still skies.
    Ponderosa pines
        softly sway
back and forth
    with my breath.
 Clusters
    of sparkling needles
        kiss my cheeks.

Sunrise

Rising sun
   over the tree tops
      paints
         patches of amber
            beneath my feet.

Brilliant stripes
   randomly
      cast on
         weathered trunks
            draw my eyes.

         A calligraphy of light.

Gift

Ah… a breath
— a pause—
another breath.
The wind sweeps
through my chest.

A flurry of leaves
snatches the light,
it falls on my canvas.

A painting is born.

Morning

New morning.
Sun-splashed dew
sprinkles
the grass,
the leaves,
my eyelashes.
Love ripples
over the bright, bright day.

Enchanted clarity.

Timeless Loving

Sharp unraveling
Shadows fading
A shower of distant stars.

Love ever deepening
Soul folding into soul
Bodies merging
The Divine dancing.

Dyad

The feel of you
wrapped around my back.
Entwined dyad,
slowly drifting away.

Our bodies
portals to infinity.

Heart Sutra

No story line
No expectation
No form
No emptiness
Just
Waves of awareness
Sparkling with moonlight
Moment by moment.

Haiku of Sorts

The heart breaks open
A thousand shards
Of mirror glass
Each
Reflecting
The clear blue sky.

Absence

Absent is the feel of your skin
The assemblage of your bones
The weight of your arms
The curves of your lips
The valley of your neck
Your separate heartbeat…

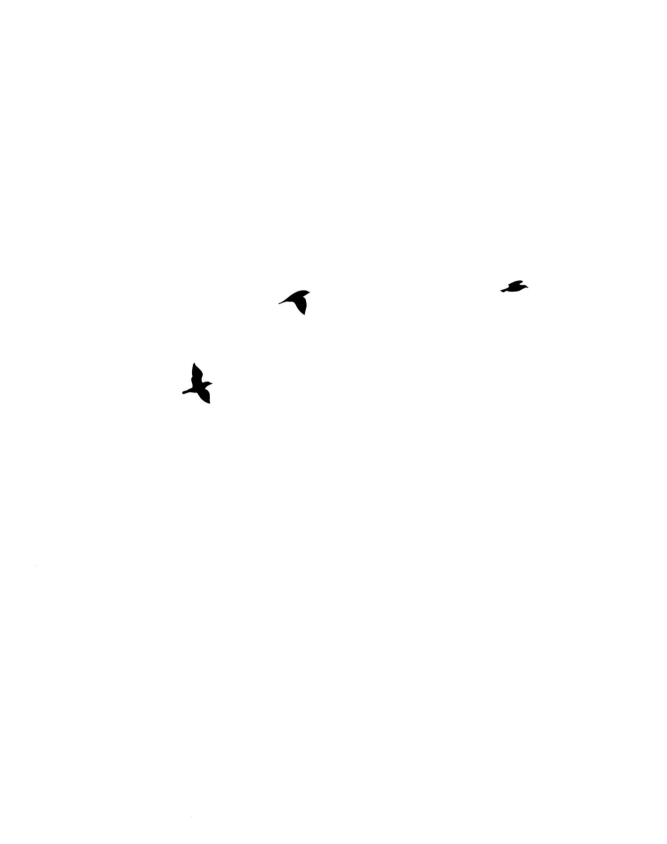

CLAY

Clad with invisible eyes,
hands stretch, pull, knead and smooth
the cool, moist earth.
The fertile matter is
both demanding and generous.
The body listens attentively.
Figures, melded with elemental spirits,
spin mysterious tales.
Winds from the four corners
gather ancient prayers.
Mitakuye Oyasin—All Our Relations,
the Lakota chant of oneness and harmony,
spires through all creation.

The Little Prince

Wisdom Goddess

The Bear

The Gatekeeper

Part Three

Small Tales

The Night I Spent with Maurice Sendak

Last night was
an unusually balmy night
for mid-November.
I stripped my bedclothes and lay
naked between the sheets.
Sometime later, I heard the coyotes.
The hills vibrated with
their high-pitched yelps, howls
and all manners of wild calls.
The coyotes were agitated.
They seemed to be running in circles,
they nibbled at the corners of my pillow,
they breathed their hurried breath under my nose,
they scratched at the bed posts and
left chaotic foot prints
on the red side rug.
The owl hooted softly,
the moon curved into a Cheshire cat's smile,
the crickets chirped, oblivious of the calendar.
And I, leaving my sleeping body warmly tucked in bed,
joined in the nocturnal carousal,
trotting joyfully with
my four-legged companions
to where the wild things are.

Shades of Green

Have you ever noticed
how many shades of green
drip from the loose limbs
of the weeping willow tree?

Have you ever noticed
how many shades of green
pool in the mossy shadow
of the gnarly oak?

Have you ever noticed
the infinite hues
at the bottom
of the shallow pond, or
on one single blade of grass?

Truly seeing
is tasting
seamless beauty.

Sounds

Ahhh, exhales the wide maple.
Hmmm, breathes in the bumble bee.
Ohhh, sighs the weary mom.
Swushh, swings the cat's angry tail.
Shshh, whispers the wind in the dry thistle.
Ommm, sings the fallen leaf.

Poised,
arms flung wide open,
I crouch
over the smooth edge
of silence.

A Cat's Tale

Though tame, my tiger cat
retains the wild and liquid stealth
of faraway jungles and
leaves amorous offerings of
mice's heads and strewn feathers
on my doorstep.

At night, never one
to observe formalities,
he pounces on my bed and wakens me
with raspy kisses on my neck and face.
But why complain?
Love is love, I think,
as I survey
the wide berth of my bed,
empty at this time of any scrumptious lovers.

So, for now, I am quite content
to navigate the night
with my feline companion,
the curled comma of his spine,
a soft punctuation to my folded body.
And who knows, we might even share
dreams of exquisitely varied scents
of earth after rain,
or of mysterious creatures hidden
among the blades of grass, the fallen leaves, the brambles.
And maybe, we will stop,
startled, face to face,
I, crouching low to the ground,
he, lost in a nocturnal reverie
about his prospective prey.

We will bow to each other like two old Zen monks
not at all fooled by our mutual disguises.

Twins

Walking backward
on our way
to the future,
shreds of remembrance
flickering
under our eyelids,
we stumbled upon
a shrouded cave,
the site
of winged desires.

There,
a binary constellation of hearts,
spiraling
inward and outward,
were spinning a spool
of enchanted filaments.
A delicate and luminous web,
woven
by diligent fingers,
stretched
across time.

Of a common accord,
holding hands,
we dropped
weightless
into
the transparent net,
becoming at last
the one
we had
always been.

Seeds of Sorrow

Seeds of sorrow
planted deep into the furrows
of the fields behind my house,
dormant,
for so long,
hard shells
protecting
the soft underbelly
of countless heartbreaks, grief,
and even agony.

An interminable winter,
so it seems,
hard crust of earth,
frozen lips.
Will Spring ever come?

A pale sun spreads a thin sheet of light
without warmth,
over the desolate terrain,
Patience is required
of all and everything.
Sleep your dreamless night,
says the world,
and wait.

When nothing more is expected,
a mockingbird is heard,
not too far away.
A deep rumbling underground,
a shiver in the veins of the naked branches
is felt even through the walls of the house.
A jagged line rips the hard skin of the seed,
a tentative shoot,
compelled,
seeks the light.

Looking through the kitchen window,
soon enough,
I see a green haze
surfing the fields,
rippling from day to day,
in the changing winds.
Then one morning,
the fields are awash
in improbable colors.

I run out of the house
and lie down between two rows of
the strange and mystifying flowers,
that have covered
the once barren landscape.
I can see the sky
in the negative spaces,
drawn by leaves and wild petals,
and
at long last,
I feel
whole
again.

Solitude

I walk
the circumference
of my being,
wearing my solitude
like a cloak of silky veils.

This weightless garment
magically reins in time.
Life's hazy contours
become saturated
with a wealth
of intricate details.

In silent stillness,
the steady beat
of our collective heart,
concealed by
humanity's incessant noise,
now reveals
what has always been there:
the enormous vastness of the world.

On the Art of Doing Nothing

In Italy it is called "dolce farniente" the oh, so exquisite practice
of doing nothing.
In France, the expression is "se la couler douce" which literally means to have it [life] flow
sweetly.
In America, thanks to the pervasive puritan influence,
it is referred to as "wasting time."
We artists, poets, visionaries have our own country,
regardless of where we live.
It is a land certainly more attuned to the French or Italian nations.
One with an anthem that glorifies
time empty of ubiquitous activities.
We know that "doing nothing" is not a luxury;
as a matter of fact, it is our very nourishment,
the air we breathe,
the warm pool where we float on our back,
contemplating the undersides of clouds.
It is the bench in our garden
where we sit,
hands folded on our lap,
deciphering the patterns of light
trapped in the shadows of the fig tree leaves,
or quietly counting how many shades of red
grace the petals of the poppies—
our ears filled
with the hum of the bees
and hummingbirds.
How many times have I lain in bed
utterly content to look out the window
at the ever changing hills, trees and sky?
The Red-tailed Hawks, who nest
in the large oak crowning the slope,
have so often lightened my heart
with their seemingly effortless flights.
So, yes, we crazy artists, poets, visionaries,
do cultivate the art of doing nothing,
which mostly requires solitude,

for if we didn't stand still
and listen with our entire being,
how could life astonish us, over and over?
Where would our Art come from?

The Little Girl

A little girl,
four or so,
curls bouncing,
skirt trailing in the breeze,
saunters across a field
of white daisies.

She pauses,
here and there,
to pick a perfect flower.
Her face,
an open sky,
smiles to the sun
and the wind
and the tiny
and not so tiny bugs.

Standing still
at the edge of the clearing,
I watch her as she comes
running toward me,
daisies held tightly
in her small hand,
their hearts of gold
spilling into mine.

Beauty

Just last weekend,
lying naked on my back,
on the sunny deck
of my favorite hot spring
while dozens of other naked bodies
were playing lazy lizards,
eager to soak in
the warmth of the bright sun,
I had a fairly empty mind
as I tend to, there.

Thoughts were far between,
floating in and out of my head,
like the puffy clouds above,
the occasional dashing bird,
the slow circling hawks,
each of them drawn in precise lines against the cerulean sky.

As it happens there was a breeze
and there was a cottonwood tree nearby.
A wild flurry of cottonwood fluff
was soon swirling all around us
as if an invisible hand had shaken one of those globes
with perfect worlds
inside their clear bubbles.

I was watching the parade
of everything
in my field of vision,
when a childhood memory resurfaced:
as a child of six or seven,
I loved to catch butterflies.
They would land on the purple clusters of flowers
of the buddleia near my house,
I would approach stealthily,
trying to catch one

oh, so softly,
inside my cupped hands.
not wanting to disturb
the delicate pigment of its intricate design,
but hoping
that the subtle flutter against my palms
would yield
the ultimate secret of beauty.

But soon,
I had to release my captive
and let it fly away.

I still find myself wanting
to capture and
hold on to beauty
in its many forms—
a sweet feeling, an extraordinary sight,
a magical moment, a perfect wisdom,
but the wind inevitably
whispers in my ear
to let everything go.
And sometimes,
as I open my hands wide,
I get a glimpse
of the unveiled world
in all its splendor,
just for a moment,
between my spread fingers.

On a Plane

Looking down
at the flocculent clouds,
their shadows cutting odd shapes
on the floor of the earth,
I imagined walking
on this wisp of a carpet,
my feet slightly sinking
into a breath of mist,
heaven smelling of the bluest sky,
or maybe lying down,
half swallowed
by the heavenly fluff,
my head filled with dreams
of arctic dragons
breathing down my neck,
their golden eyes reflecting
my reclining body.

The Guardian

Baby red fox
curled around my spine,
bushy tail tucked
beneath my pelvis,
the triangle of your face
rests against my womb,
pointy nose over paws.

Anubis,
guarding a strange domain of
half buried tombstones
and crumbling cherubs,
you know
when old grief
needs tending to.

Sharp teeth
nibbling at my soft tissues,
remind me that,
hidden
in the tawny shadows,
lies the true secret of joy.

Windows

I like to write poems the old-fashioned way, a pen in my right hand, coursing on the lined page of my hardcover notebook. The letters scamper on the paper, sometimes surprising me with improbable associations that delight the imagination.

As I sit on my bed this morning, somewhere in Paris, twelfth arrondissement, high above the ground, and wonder what to write to you, whom I left across an ocean, I give myself my own advice— step into your direct experience at this very moment.

So I look out the window,
as poets tend to do,
and notice the straight alignment
of other windows
across the courtyard,
each boasting its distinct personality.
This one, with its blinds half rolled,
has a sleepy face.
That one hides behind drawn curtains.
Another peers at me with candid openness,
nothing blocking the view.
And then again there are those
with lace trimmings
cutting triangles
in each corner
or drawing twin verticals
down their sides.

I hear the clamor
of children's voices
down below,
school is out.
The buildings stretch their walls around the court,
their outline crowned
by a piece of sky,
brimming with that unique Parisian light,
bright yet diffuse.

I wonder if the people
behind those squares of glass
are letting the world in
or closing the world out?

Is the woman, with the expressive face,
who unconsciously tucks a strand of hair
behind her ear,
thinking about the return of the swallows
from far away lands?
Or about the solitary cup of tea
waiting on the wooden table?

How about the old man,
sitting on a chair
parallel to the window,
lost in a world of memories.
Is he remembering
how much, as a young boy,
he loved to jump
with both feet
into the puddles
after the rain?

Do these people know
that they are traveling in the same
stone-crafted ship,
sailing through time,
destination unknown,
on a blue planet
orbiting the sun?
All sharing the same joys, tears, heartaches, love, hate, hurts...

Their lives flowing like a river
turning back on itself.

Last Night

Waking up in my tent,
I gazed at the lacy tree tops
and speckled sky,
through the two meshed triangles
over my head.

I listened to the water of
the nearby creek,
its sound coming closer and closer
till the rushing stream
entered my left shoulder
and coursed across my chest.
My ribs became smooth river stones,
thirsty for the
cool and swift caress
of the joyous water.

A child cried in the distance.
The stars slowly faded into a lighter sky
and I, wrapped gently
in the folds of the coming dawn,
fell back asleep.

Traveling Mercies

I was on a plane, US Air, Las Vegas to San Francisco, seat 17 A, near the window. I had just left you and was feeling sad and somewhat forlorn.

The young man next to me had a beautiful face, the color of the smoothest blend of apricot, cream and espresso. He hadn't lowered the armrest, so we sat shoulder to shoulder in a most comfortable way, as if the sides of our arms had known each other forever — old friends aligned in a companionable silence, punctuated by a rare informal comment, the subject of the inordinate desert heat bound to come up at some point in the conversation.

We were reading our respective books. His, I noticed, on the Templar knights; mine, "Traveling Mercies" by Anne Lamott, one of my favorite local writers. Traveling mercies is what the old Black folks, at her church, say when one of them goes off — love the journey, God be with you, come home safe and sound.

His delicate fingers alternately rested and turned the pages at regular intervals. A gentle and peaceful energy emanated from his being, and by and by, I started to feel comforted and soothed by the light and warm pressure alongside our parallel arms, and my heart seemed to settle. Angels come in many forms, I thought, as I glanced out the window at the landscape of clouds.

A blue haze had spread over the land, so that earth and water were indistinguishable, and it looked like we were traveling above the ice cap, snow piled in little mounds, a polar bear possibly striding along, pausing near one of those blue holes in the hope of catching a sleepy fish.

As we started our final descent, I asked my companion about his book. I told him about mine, and in that short time, we managed to exchange some very intimate ideas. It turned out that he admired the Dalai Lama, my hero and inspiration in human kindness, and was following his comments on Twitter. As I had sensed, this young man was a lovely person-mature, sweet and smart and to my surprise, a corporate lawyer.

"Traveling mercies to you," I wished him silently when we parted. Thank you for lightening my heart; may we indeed love the journey and all go home safe and sound.

Summer

I sit in the car.
No words come to mind,
only
sounds, light, colors....
Trees,
green upon green,
never the same,
stamp dotted shapes
against the light straw
of our scorched summer.
Hazy skies,
slightly smelling
of smoke,
are silent reminders
of planetary changes.
Please, Mother Earth,
I pray,
let me pour
tears of joy and pain,
enough to quench
your thirsty skin.
Let me lie
face down
on your back
and not move
or turn
until the crow says so.

Sorrow

Under the eaves of my shoulder blades
sorrow has gathered,
displacing one or two of my ribs
out of their furrows.

This is not the
harsh kind of grief
that stops you
dead in your tracks,
holding your sides
gasping for breath.

No, this is a quiet sort of sorrow,
a lake,
barely a ripple when I move.
In it, reversed,
the green triangles of the pines,
the mountain tops,
the passing clouds,
the arrowhead of the Canadian geese.

On the shore,
a singular figure
watches me,
waits for me?
I see her
when I venture out,
floating on my delicate craft.
I peer into that bottomless lake,
trying to make sense
of the ever changing patterns
of viridian shadows.

She sometimes waves at me,
urges me on,
trusting, knowing
that I will reach the other shore
in this life
or the next one
it doesn't matter which.

Meanwhile, I remember
to breathe,
to take in the beauty
as it shines
equally on the whole world.

Surprise

I thought I knew
what I wanted from life,
surely from love,
a soul mate,
a lover,
a companion,
to share my every day
to share my every night.

But it seems not so.
A couple of lovers have crossed
my meandering path,
each extraordinary
in his own way,
drawing out a sharp breath,
a song,
a graceful limbed tree,
a tide unseen…

Yet,
when they return
to their daily tasks,
leaving me once again alone,
I find myself happy
[almost exuberant]
at the thought of stepping back
into the circle of my solitary days,
the stretch of uncharted dawns,
the slow moving river of time,
its final destination unknown.

I swim in the silence of my empty house
and I say to myself:
I have a life,
it is full,
it is rich,
I am complete.

Grief

No stranger to grief
I have learned
to sit,
over time,
with its sharp edges.

The brutal truth
of the finite
string of hours
assigned to
all we love,
still makes me gasp.
Yet, nowadays,
I can savor
a quiet cup of tea
with this,
once,
dreaded visitor.

The leaves unfurling
in the amber brew
draw the shape
of my curled body,
sorrowful
at your absence,
lying in the imprint
you left
in the bent grass.

They reflect
the weary faces
of loved and
unknown ones
who battle
disease and disaster.

They tell of the gentle life
of my younger cat
who died in my arms
only last week,
his joyous and valiant spirit
now a wisp of smoke
absorbed by the clouds.

The tea leaves
slowly float
to the bottom
of my cup,
to whisper
a quiet Kaddish
for all those departed.

A thousand times,
our hearts shatter,
a thousand times
we find reasons to love again.

A thousand times,
we shed our tears,
a thousand times,
we find reasons to laugh.

How courageous
we are,
we, fragile voyagers
suspended in space,
aboard
our small mother ship.

Our passage here
all too brief,
to withhold
or be miserly
in the expression of our love.

If grief has taught me anything
it is to soften,
to be humble,
knowing that
each instant,
many share
the same anguish.

Our hearts are threaded
in an unending
chain of compassion,
leaving only a prayer
for merciful awareness
to color our journey
and bring us
safely home,
back to ourselves.

The Lighthouse

Swirling winds
spin me
in wild circles.
Low clouds
conceal the world.
I am lost
at sea,
on a light vessel,
adrift.

Still, spiraling
out of control,
I suddenly
catch a glimpse
of an orbiting glint
that pierces
the opaque gray
shrouding me.

This luminous dot
slowly anchors me to
a still center.
The wind quiets—
a pause.

In the eye of the storm,
the lucent shell of existence
opens.

A Twins' Tale

Did we burst forth
borne by the rushing waters
of our mother's womb?
Or emerge fully grown
from this ancient king's forehead?
Or maybe still
spring from a thought
yet unformed?

Holding each other
in a tight embrace,
we tumbled, head first,
into the cupped hands
of slightly worn heroes
biding their time
till it was time again.

The road, a forked tongue,
carried you over here,
ushered me over there,
miles away, years apart.
only the body remembered.
Memories lay, encrypted
in double helixes spiraling silently,
waiting to reverse time
and reconstitute
the seamless, smooth oval of light
we once were.

My Cats

The older cat likes to drape himself across my neck; a luxurious stole of living flesh, purring into my throat the simple facts of his contented love.

More often than not, he licks my face with the rasp of his tongue – a bittersweet sensation.

When I sit at my desk, doing this and that, the younger one, a clown in disguise, leaps onto my lap – a flash of liquid fur – and melts into my knees, a silly grin on his face.

More often than not, he runs toward me when he hears my car pull in, greeting me with his distinctive, most awful sounding meow.

More often than not, I bury my face into this one or that one's soft body and long to become its blood and bones.

Things Lost

The dark silhouetted trees
stand guard
over my troubled sleep.
The wind exhales
through their limbs,
stirring splashes of
drifting moonlight
that cling
to the folds of
their curled leaves.

I am dreaming of
all things lost.
Their absence
traverses the hollow of
my bones,
whistling
a faded tune.

The owl, intent and still,
peers
through the darkness.
He suddenly dives
into the underbrush.
I feel
his sharp talons
snatching
some small life
from its
nocturnal activity.

Borne by
the choppy waters
of my unconscious,
I toss and turn.

And wake up
from my fitful sleep.

Dawn steals through
the slats of the blinds
pale and cold.
The Canadian geese,
flying overhead,
call to each other
like every morning.
The ghost of doubt
wavers under my eyelids.

Then you call,
and in your voice
I hear
that, for the moment,
things that were lost
have been found.

The Soul of a Poet

The soul of a poet,
like a chrysalis,
waits patiently
for the encoded clues,
dreaming of weightless flight,
of exquisite colors,
of scented encounters.

Without warning,
the reverie comes to an end.
The wings unfold,
a startling show of beauty,
the poet is born.
Carried by the soft wind,
he flies into the light, into the rain,
into the mossy shadows,
pausing, here and there,
to love
a unique flower.

Geckos Like Sweets

A cohort of geckos
has taken residence
in my Balinese-style dwelling.
Open on three sides,
it is suspended
midway from the ground,
not quite to the top
of the opulent trees.

Naked, most of the time,
I go about my day
in dolce farniente,
wrapped in tropical mist.
The breeze on my skin
a flutter - a caress - a kiss.

At night, the coquis,
tiny, sonorous frogs,
weave a tapestry of sounds,
which hangs
from the walls of my dreams
infusing Morpheus' offerings.

The throaty roar of the surf,
along with Pele's fiery breath
and the clatter of the palms,
draw a precise graph
of invisible frequencies.
Earth - Water - Air - Fire,
all elements allied,
conspire to unravel and
reconstitute my being
in their nocturnal travail.
Trusting, I surrender
to this erratic makeover.

As dawn lightens the sky,
a symphony of bird calls
gradually reshapes the soundscape.
I wake up to find
my gecko friends,
happily licking the bottle of honey
or burrowing their tongue
in the opening of a banana.
What simple wisdom,
I think to myself,
savoring a sweet thing
when it comes your way.
So I get up,
fully intending
to follow in their footsteps
and dance my life
through another day
in paradise.

A Nothing Day

Today was a nothing kind of day
nothing urgent to do,
nowhere to go,
my calendar blank,
the day
stretching lazily in front of me.
I tended to simple things:
letting the dog out,
feeding the cats,
calling my sister,
drinking coffee,
typing poems,
answering emails,
driving my son around,
going for a walk,
coming home,
cooking,
eating,
cleaning,
taking a bath,
writing this.
All the while feeling
oh, so peaceful and happy.

Nothing days—
life's quiet gifts.

The Young Girl

Bare legs passing through
on the way to real life,
her back straight,
her head held high,
in spite of the tears
behind her eyes,

she raises her hands
to catch the last rays
of the setting sun.
Red light drips
from her fanned fingers
and pools around
her bony shoulders.

A bright yellow crunchy
holds her unruly curls
in a dark ponytail,
which moves up and down
with each step.
If you didn't see her face
you might think
she was just hurrying
to a simple rendezvous
with her friends.

But she can't quite hide
the tightness of her mouth,
the two vertical lines
etched
between her eyebrows,
her eyes too bright.

Inside she feels
she might collapse
or fold like one of those chairs
her parents bring out
when there are more guests
than usual.

She keeps on walking
deliberately
although she has no idea
where her feet are taking her.
She inhales sharply
when it seems too much
to contain it all.

Who said that first love
couldn't be that serious,
that only with age
could one feel so profoundly?
She shakes her head
at the folly of it
and slows her steps.

Finally stopping
under a wide oak,
she falls on her knees
on the fresh cut grass
and lets the tears come.

They fall silently
on the back of her folded hands,
and on the yellow leaves,
dotting the brilliant colors with
tiny transparent pools
of crushed possibilities.

Made in the USA
Middletown, DE
26 February 2023

25537121R00058